DATE DUE

FEB 13 '70			
MAY 21 '70			
FEB 2			
FE 24 '72			
OC 17 '74			
DE 5 74			
SE 21 '76			
MR 14 '78			
MR 16 '78			
MAY 1 1 1987			
GAYLORD			PRINTED IN U.S.A.

BEGINNING SOCIAL STUDIES

FOLLETT

Library of Congress Catalog Card Number: 63-9618

123456789

Our National Anthem

by Nicholas Georgiady
and Louis Romano

ILLUSTRATED BY GERALD McCANN

Follett Publishing Company
Chicago

A national anthem is a song that is sung all over a country. It is a song that makes people proud of their country.

Sometimes the song is about a hero or a
fight for freedom. Most national anthems tell
something about the history of the country.

5

Our own national anthem, "The Star-Spangled Banner," was written when our country was new. It was not very many years after the Revolutionary War, which freed us from English rule.

The young United States of America was at war with England again. This war was called the War of 1812.

Some English ships had sailed into Chesapeake Bay. The English took an American prisoner, a Doctor Beanes. He was held on one of the English ships.

A lawyer who was a friend of Dr. Beanes went to the English ship. The lawyer's name was Francis Scott Key. Another American, Colonel John Skinner, went with Key. They hoped to get the English admiral to free Doctor Beanes.

After they talked, the English admiral
said he would free Doctor Beanes. But he said
none of the Americans could go right away.

The English were about to attack Fort
McHenry in Baltimore Harbor. They would not
let Francis Scott Key and the others go until
the battle was over.

From a ship's deck, Key and his friends
looked on as the battle started. They could
see the Stars and Stripes flying over Fort
McHenry. It was a big flag, thirty by forty-two
feet. Even though the ship they were on was far
from the fort, they could still see the flag.

Cannons from the English ships fired on
Fort McHenry. From the fort the American
cannons fired back.

Francis Scott Key kept watching the big
red, white, and blue flag. He knew that when
the flag was lowered, all would be lost. The
English would have won the battle.

The Americans watched the flag until it
was too dark to see it. They stayed awake all
night. Cannons roared and shells flew through
the air. Rockets were fired that lit up the sky.

Very late that night the roar of cannons stopped. But Key and his friends did not know what that meant. Had Fort McHenry surrendered? Or had the English given up the attack?

There was no way for them to know. There was nothing to do but wait.

As the dawn came, the three men strained their eyes to see if the Stars and Stripes was still flying. It was misty and smoky, so they could not see well.

At last the mist cleared for a moment. Key and the other men saw a wonderful sight. Over the walls of Fort McHenry floated the Stars and Stripes.

The flag was torn by shells and bullets, but it still flew proudly. The Americans had not lost the fight.

Francis Scott Key was filled with joy. He
wanted to write down the wonderful feeling he
had as he saw his country's flag still flying over
the fort.

He took out an old letter and quickly wrote these words on the back of it:

"Oh! say, can you see
    by the dawn's early light,
What so proudly we hailed
    at the twilight's last gleaming?"

He remembered how he had watched the flag
the evening before. He wrote more words:

> "Whose broad stripes and bright stars,
>   thro' the perilous fight,
> O'er the ramparts we watched,
>   were so gallantly streaming?"

19

Key thought about the long night of battle.
He wrote more words:

> "And the rockets' red glare,
>> the bombs bursting in air,
> Gave proof thro' the night
>> that our flag was still there.

> Oh! say, does that star-spangled
>> banner yet wave
> O'er the land of the free and the
>> home of the brave?"

He remembered the joy in his heart when he
saw the American flag still flying. He tried to
find just the right words to say how he felt.

The English admiral kept his word. He let
the three Americans go as soon as the battle was
over. Key and his friends went back to Baltimore.
There Key wrote down more verses telling his
feelings about our flag and our country.

All the verses were printed, and people
saw them and liked them. Soon the verses were
being sung to the tune of an older popular song.
The older song was called "Adams and Liberty."
The music fit Key's verses very well.

Soon people were singing "The Star-Spangled
Banner." They kept on singing it as years passed.

Bands played it in many places. Everyone
knew and sang "The Star-Spangled Banner."

But it was not until 1931 that Congress
adopted Francis Scott Key's song as our national
anthem.

Today "The Star-Spangled Banner" is sung
in classrooms from Maine to Hawaii. It is sung
in assembly programs. It is sung at many
different kinds of public meetings.

Before the start of a football game or a
baseball game, our national anthem is often
sung or played.

Everyone stands when "The Star-Spangled
Banner" is played.

When the national anthem is played, but
the flag is not shown, everyone should face
toward the music.

People in uniform salute at the first note and keep on saluting until the last note.

All other people stand up straight while the national anthem is sung. Men take off their hats.

We are proud of our national anthem.
The words remind us of all the people
who have worked to make this country great.

They remind us of all the people who have given their lives to make this country free.

They remind us that we must all do everything we can for our country. We must keep America strong and free.

THE *Star-Spangled Banner*

Oh! say, can you see, by the dawn's early light,

What so proudly we hailed at the twilight's

last gleaming?

Whose broad stripes and bright stars, thro' the

perilous fight,

O'er the ramparts we watched were so gallantly

streaming?

And the rockets' red glare, the bombs bursting

in air,

Gave proof thro' the night that our flag was

still there.

Oh! say, does that star-spangled banner yet wave

O'er the land of the free and the home

of the brave?

On the shore, dimly seen thro' the mist of

the deep,

Where the foe's haughty host in dread silence

reposes,

What is that which the breeze, o'er the

towering steep,

As it fitfully blows, half conceals, half
    discloses?
Now it catches the gleam of the morning's first
    beam,
In full glory reflected, now shines on the
    stream.
'Tis the star-spangled banner. Oh! long may
    it wave
O'er the land of the free and the home
    of the brave!

Oh! thus be it ever, when free men shall stand
Between their loved homes and the war's
    desolation!
Blest with vict'ry and peace, may the Heav'n-
    rescued land
Praise the Pow'r that hath made and preserved
    us a nation.
Then conquer we must, when our cause it is just,
And this be our motto, "In God is our trust."
And the star-spangled banner in triumph
    shall wave
O'er the land of the free and the home
    of the brave.

Follett Beginning Social Studies Books

Follett Beginning Social Studies books contain accurate, up-to-date information about our world—its history and geography, its people and their ways of life. These books are designed to provide pleasure in reading and to give children the information they need to enrich their lives and their school work.

Follett Beginning Social Studies books are written for the primary grades. They are completely illustrated. They cover a wide range of subjects, adding interest to the familiar and shedding light on the unfamiliar.

Our National Anthem

Understandings Developed in This Book

What a National Anthem Is.

Children will gain a new appreciation of what a national anthem is and what it means to the people of a country.

How "The Star-Spangled Banner" Was Written.

Francis Scott Key wrote the song at a time when he felt his country was in danger. The words express his great joy and relief when he saw the American flag still flying, as well as his faith and pride in his country.

When It Became Our National Anthem.

It was officially adopted by Congress in 1931, but it had been recognized as our national anthem long before that.

What We Do When "The Star-Spangled Banner" is played or sung .

Everyone stands up, and men remove their hats. People in uniform salute.

Words That May Be New

national	Fort McHenry	Congress
anthem	Baltimore Harbor	adopted
history	cannons	Maine
Revolutionary War	surrendered	Hawaii
English	attack	assembly
Chesapeake Bay	strained	public
Francis Scott Key	printed	uniform
admiral	popular	salute